AF326705

The Purring Horizon :
Whispers Beyond the Visible

The Purring Horizon: Whispers Beyond the Visible
is a quiet exploration of presence, perception, and the
subtle intelligence of cats – where their ordinary actions
reveal hidden gifts, and their smallest gestures become
gateways into awareness.

Each page presents a poem that opens a felt doorway,
an art journaling prompt that allows the experience to
take form, a gift drawn from the quiet wisdom of cats, a
message of awareness that gently reorients perception,
and a thought for your ears that invites us to listen to
what cannot be spoken.

Together, they form a subtle practice – a way of entering
the moment more fully, guided by the quiet intelligence
that cats embody without effort.

Written and illustrated by Nina Pragati who weaves
poetry, visual art, and reflective prompts into meditative
experiences, inviting readers to find beauty, softness,
and meaning in the everyday.

Edited with care and quiet precision by Veeraj, whose
sensitivity to rhythm, tone, and meaning has helped
refine these reflections into their truest form.

This book is a work of reflective and creative expression. All characters, imagery, and interpretations are presented as symbolic and philosophical explorations of lived experience.

Title: The Purring Horizon: Whispers Beyond the Visible
Author and Artist: Nina Pragati Chaudhry
Editor: Veeraj Chaudhry
First Edition, 2026
Published by Rasa Forever.

With dedication to the enduring flow of feeling, presence, and aesthetic experience that lives within and beyond all forms.

The following pages are an invitation to return to
something already present within you –
something that does not need to be improved, only
noticed.

If there is a horizon here, it is not something you move
toward. It is something that moves with you,
expanding, softening, purring just beyond the edges
of thought. You may begin anywhere.

Table of Contents

The Gift of Quiet Companionship

A cat weaves the afternoon
into a sunlit fold
as if time were cloth,
and softness its comfort.
They chase invisible things
like midnight philosophers of light,
and then they sleep as though they've solved
a question we never asked.
Their gift is this:
to sit beside you without fixing,
to stay without speaking,
to love without asking why.

Hear Hear
Soft purr, steady
a heartbeat outside my own,
teaching me to rest.

Art Journaling Prompt
Paint or draw a small space of comfort
a sofa, a porch swing, a lap.
Let something unseen be present:
a shadow, a breath, a feeling.
How does companionship live
when no words are spoken?

Message of Awareness
Not everything needs to be solved
some things only ask to be witnessed with gentleness.

The Gift of Playful Presence

A cat invents a universe
from a crumpled receipt
skidding across galaxies of tile,
declaring joy without permission.
They leap like punctuation marks
sudden, exact, unapologetic
turning ordinary rooms
into bright interruptions.
Their gift is this:
to enter the moment completely,
to treat small things as infinite,
to remember delight without reason.

Hear Hear

Tap - rustle - leap
laughter hides in small sounds,
waiting to be found.

Art Journaling Prompt

Create a page using scraps - paper bits, threads, wrappers.
Arrange them into something unexpected and lively.
Let your composition feel spontaneous, even mischievous.
What happens when you allow "insignificant" things
to become the center?

Message of Awareness

Joy does not require importance
it arrives when you stop ranking your moments.

The Gift of Sacred Boundaries

A cat draws a circle
no one else can see
a quiet perimeter of whiskers and will,
where presence is chosen, not owed.
They leave mid-stroke, mid-touch, mid-thrust,
unapologetic as the moon slipping through clouds,
returning only when the heart
feels like a safe place again.
Their gift is this:
to say yes with the whole body,
and no without explanation
a dignity that does not waver.

Hear Hear

Pause... soft retreat
silence draws its own line,
held without a word.

Art Journaling Prompt

Draw or paint a boundary as a living form
not a wall, but something breathing:
a halo, a forest edge, a shifting tide.
Where is it firm? Where is it permeable?
Let your page show both protection and invitation.

Message of Awareness

You are allowed to step away
and still be whole.

The Gift of Curiosity

A cat tilts the world sideways -
peering into cups, corners,
the quiet behind curtains,
as if reality were only half-finished.
They follow threads no one else sees,
listening to the grammar of shadows,
asking questions with their paws
instead of needing answers.
Their gift is this:
to wander without conclusion,
to let wonder be enough,
to trust the unknown as a doorway.

Hear Hear

Whisper... scratch... still
a question curls in the air,
never needing end.

Art Journaling Prompt

Create a page of "unanswered things"
draw doorways, tunnels, tiny openings.
Let some lead nowhere, some overlap.
Think of these as questions, not statements.
What does your curiosity look like without needing closure?

Message of Awareness

Not knowing is not emptiness
it is space where new seeing begins.

The Gift of Soft Landing

A cat falls like a secret
the earth already knows
bones remembering air,
feet translating trust into return.
From windows, from missteps, from heights of thought,
they descend without drama,
as if gravity were not a force
but a conversation they agreed to.
Their gift is this:
to begin again mid-fall,
to meet the ground as an ally,
to land without breaking the moment.

Hear Hear
Drop - hush - arrival,
the ground opens like arms,
nothing truly lost.

Art Journaling Prompt
Create a layered page that begins in chaos
fast marks, drips, torn edges
then gently bring parts of it into balance.
Add soft shapes or grounding forms beneath.
Where does your page "land," and how does it hold you?

Message of Awareness
Falling is not failure
it is a movement toward where you can stand again.

The Gift of Ritual

A cat returns to the same sun patch
as if it were a shrine
circling, settling,
honoring light like an old friend.
They groom the hours into order,
licking time into stillness,
repeating small ceremonies
that stitch the day together.
Their gift is this:
to make the ordinary sacred,
to return again and again
until presence becomes prayer.

Hear Hear

Step... pause... return
a circle hums softly,
holding the day still.

Art Journaling Prompt

Choose one small daily act - tea, walking, breathing.
Create a page that repeats a simple shape or symbol
to reflect this rhythm.
Let the repetition become calming, almost meditative.
What changes when you treat routine as ritual?

Message of Awareness

Consistency is not dullness
it is where meaning quietly deepens.

The Gift of Hidden Worlds

A cat disappears
into places that do not announce themselves
behind curtains, beneath beds,
inside the pause between footsteps.
They vanish without leaving,
reappearing like a thought remembered late,
carrying dust of unseen corners
as if they've traveled somewhere sacred.
Their gift is this:
to slip between the visible and the felt,
to remind us there are rooms
inside every ordinary moment.

Hear Hear

Faint rustle... gone
a world moves just out of sight,
breathing in the hush.

Art Journaling Prompt

Create a page with layers you can partially hide
folds, flaps, translucent paper.
Let some images peek through, others stay concealed.
What do you choose to reveal, and what remains a quiet
world within?

Message of Awareness

Not everything meant for you
is meant to be seen all at once.

The Gift of Unapologetic Rest

A cat sleeps in the middle of everything
conversations, sunlight, unfinished days
as if rest were not an afterthought
but the center of being alive.
They stretch like a quiet truth,
claiming space without permission,
closing their eyes to the world
and trusting it will still be there.
Their gift is this:
to stop without "earning" it,
to soften without guilt,
to rest as a right, not a reward.

Hear Hear
Slow breath... soften
the world hums quietly on,
while I drift within.

Art Journaling Prompt
Create a page with soft textures -
pastels, smudges, blurred edges.
Let forms dissolve rather than define.
Add a space that feels like a pause
a breath, a place to lie down.
Where does your page invite you to rest?

Message of Awareness
You do not have to finish everything
to deserve stillness.

The Gift of Sudden Grace

A cat becomes lightning
for no reason at all
a blur through stillness,
a streak across the ordinary.
One moment, silence
the next, a dance of instinct and air,
as if joy struck the body
before thought could follow.
Their gift is this:
to move when the moment calls,
to trust the body's knowing,
to let energy speak without apology.

Hear Hear

Flash - soft echo fades
a moment splits into light,
then rests again, whole.

Art Journaling Prompt

Create a page with one sudden, bold movement
a swift brushstroke, a splash, a tear across paper.
Let the rest remain quiet or minimal.
Where does your page come alive in a single instant?

Message of Awareness

Not all clarity arrives slowly
some truths flash through you all at once.

The Gift of Gentle Attention

A cat watches the smallest shift
a flicker in the air,
a dust mote changing direction,
the almost-nothing of a moving world.
They sit inside the moment
as if it were vast
eyes wide with a quiet devotion
to what most would pass by.
Their gift is this:
to notice without needing more,
to let subtlety be enough,
to honor the barely-there.

Hear Hear

Soft shift... almost still
something small becomes the world,
held in quiet sight.

Art Journaling Prompt

Create a page using very light marks
fine lines, faint colors, barely visible shapes.
Work slowly, almost whispering onto the page.
What emerges when you attend to the smallest details?

Message of Awareness

Attention is a form of love
especially when given to what is easily overlooked.

The Gift of Quiet Courage

A cat walks the edge of everything
ledges, unknown rooms,
the thin line between fear and curiosity
tail steady as a question mark.
They step where certainty ends,
not because they are fearless,
but because something inside them
trusts the next moment enough.
Their gift is this:
to move gently into the unsure,
to let courage be soft,
and still go forward.

Hear Hear

Step... pause... step
the unknown opens slowly,
and I enter still.

Art Journaling Prompt

Create a page that begins with a blank edge.
Let your marks slowly move inward from that edge
hesitant at first, then more confident.
What does your version of "stepping into the
unknown" look like visually?

Message of Awareness

Courage does not have to be loud
it can be a quiet step that continues.

The Gift of Returning

A cat leaves without farewell
into alleys of thought,
into private constellations
gone as if absence were natural.
And then, without announcement,
they are back
a soft weight, a familiar warmth,
as if distance had only deepened the thread.
Their gift is this:
to wander without losing the bond,
to return without needing to explain,
to trust that love can stretch and still hold.

Hear Hear

A gentle thud
presence finds its way in,
as if never lost.

Art Journaling Prompt

Create a page in two parts.
Divide the space in a way that feels natural to you.
Let one area remain open, quiet, and uncluttered.
Let the other gather texture, warmth, and depth.
Use marks, color, or materials to build contrast.
Gently connect them with a subtle line, or shape

Message of Awareness

Distance does not always break connection
sometimes it reveals what quietly remains.

The Gift of Soft Power

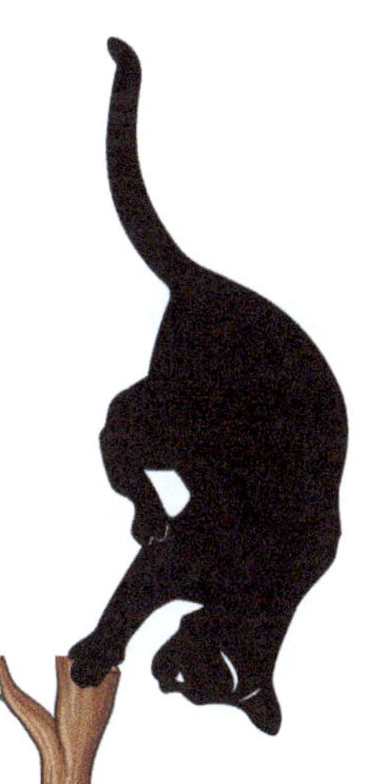

A cat does not command the room
yet the room rearranges itself
around their quiet gravity,
as if presence alone were enough.
They do not chase attention,
they let it arrive
drawn by something wordless,
something steady and self-held.
Their gift is this:
to be, without performing,
to influence, without force,
to hold space, without noise.

Hear Hear

Still... soft pull inward
silence shapes the space around,
without ever trying.

Art Journaling Prompt

Create a page with one central form.
Let everything else subtly respond to it
lighter marks, softer colors, gentle movements.
How does your page shift around a stable center?

Message of Awareness

True presence does not demand
it gathers.

The Gift of Invisible Threads

A cat knows where you are
without looking
as if something unseen
maps your movement in the air.
They arrive just before your thought
turns into need,
settling beside you
like a quiet answer already waiting.
Their gift is this:
to feel the subtle connections,
to move along what cannot be named,
to trust the thread beneath the surface.

Hear Hear

Soft step... Hard step
something knew before I did,
and met me fully.

Art Journaling Prompt

Create a page using lines that weave and intersect
some bold, some barely visible.
Let them connect shapes or spaces without explaining why.
Where do your invisible threads lead?

Message of Awareness

Not all connection is visible
some of the deepest bonds are simply felt.

The Gift of Becoming Small

A cat folds itself
into impossibly tiny spaces
a bowl, a box, a shadow
as if the world expands
when you choose to take less of it.
They disappear into corners
not to hide,
but to fit gently
within what is already there.
Their gift is this:
to take up only what is needed,
to soften the edges of self,
to belong without overflowing.

Hear Hear

Soft curl... held close
the world grows wide around me,
as I take less space.

Art Journaling Prompt

Create a very small composition in one corner of your page.
Leave the rest empty.
Let your marks be delicate, contained, intentional.
What shifts when you allow space to be larger than you?

Message of Awareness

You do not always need to expand
sometimes presence deepens when you become small.

The Gift of Trusting Instinct

A cat pauses mid-step
listening to something beneath sound,
a current that does not speak
yet asks to be followed.
They turn without reason,
refuse what looks inviting,
choosing without explainations
because knowing lives deeper than thought.
Their gift is this:
to trust the first quiet signal,
to honor the body's whisper,
to move before doubt arrives.

Hear Hear

Pause... turn... silence
a path reveals itself,
before thought can speak.

Art Journaling Prompt

Begin your page without planning
close your eyes and make the first mark.
Then let each next mark respond only to feeling, not logic.
What emerges when you follow instinct instead of design?

Message of Awareness

Your inner knowing does not need permission –
it only asks that you listen before you question.

The Gift of Sacred Timing

A cat waits longer than a moment
watching the invisible shift
before movement becomes inevitable.
They do not rush the leap,
nor linger after it is done
each action placed
exactly where it belongs.
Even hunger becomes a rhythm,
even stillness a preparation
as if time were not passing,
but unfolding with them.
Their gift is this:
to act when the moment ripens,
to wait without restlessness,
to trust the unseen becoming.

Hear Hear
Still... still... then swift
time opens like a doorway,
exactly on cue.

Art Journaling Prompt
Create a page in stages - pause between each mark.
Let one layer dry, settle, or feel complete before adding
the next. Where does patience change your composition?

Message of Awareness
Not everything is meant to happen now
some things are found at the right moment.

The Gift of Silent Listening

A cat hears what is not spoken
the weight beneath a voice,
the tremor behind stillness,
the quiet that gathers before tears.
They sit without interrupting,
ears turned to the unseen,
as if listening were an act
that could hold the whole room together.
No advice, no fixing
only presence that witnesses what moves
beneath the surface of words.
Their gift is this:
to receive without answering,
to hear without shaping,
to listen until something softens.

Hear Hear

Hush... held... echo
a silence listens back to me,
gentle and aware.

Art Journaling Prompt

Create a page while listening
to a sound, a piece of music, or silence itself.
Let your marks respond to what you hear, not what you see.
How does listening guide your hand in a new way?

Message of Awareness

To truly listen is to make space
and in that space, something begins to heal.

The Gift of Lightness

A cat lands without a sound
as if the world agreed
to hold them softly.
They carry no weight
beyond what is needed,
no story heavier than the step.
Even their mischief dissolves quickly,
like laughter that refuses to linger
nothing clings, nothing insists.
Their gift is this:
to move without burden,
to release without effort,
to let each moment remain light.

Hear Hear

Reverberating steps,
gravity gives in,
there is only air.

Art Journaling Prompt

Create airy strokes with minimal pressure on your surface.
Hold your tool lightly, letting it skim rather than press.
Allow each mark to feel weightless, as if it could lift off the page.
Leave space between strokes so breath can move through the
composition. Let your hand soften, releasing effort and control

Message of Awareness

Not everything needs to be carried
some things can be set down as you go.

The Gift of Private Joy

A cat plays when no one is watching
batting at nothing,
leaping for reasons
that belong only to the moment.
No audience, no applause
just a secret delight
folded into quiet corners,
touched only by impulse.
They do not wait to be noticed
to begin their happiness,
nor measure it by who understands.
Their gift is this:
to enjoy without display,
to own one's own joy,
to be whole, always.

Hear Hear

Faint thud... soft spin
laughter lives in hidden rooms,
just for itself.

Art Journaling Prompt

Create something you will not show anyone.
Let it be strange, playful, imperfect.
Hide parts of it, layer over it, keep it just for you.
What does your creativity become when it doesn't hide?

Message of Awareness

Your joy does not need witnessing
to be real.

The Gift of Letting Go

A cat releases what it holds
a toy, a moment, a place in the sun
without turning back
to check if it should have stayed.
They do not archive the past
in corners of their body,
nor replay what has already passed
through their quiet hours.
What leaves, leaves
as naturally as a stretch,
as easily as sleep arrives
Their gift is this:
to unclench without effort,
to trust the next moment enough
to release the one before.

Hear Hear

Loose... whoosh... release
what I no longer carry
makes room for breath.

Art Journaling Prompt

Create a page, then gently remove something
erase, tear, cover, or wash it away.
Let the absence become part of the composition.
What shifts when you allow something to leave?

Message of Awareness

Holding on is not always strength
sometimes it is the refusal to move with life.

42

Afterword

The gestures of the cat
its stillness, its instinct, its timing
are not separate from the deeper currents
that shape all living experience.
They are expressions of something elemental.
Fire in the sudden leap.
Earth in the grounded rest.
Water in the fluid adaptation.
Air in the subtle awareness.
Ether in the quiet space that holds it all.

Rasa Forever

Acknowledgments

To the cats – seen and unseen, known and unknown – whose presence shaped these pages, and whose quiet ways revealed more than instruction ever could. Each gesture, each pause, each return became a form of teaching that asked only to be noticed.

To Veeraj, for the care, clarity, and sensitivity brought to this work. Your editing allowed it to arrive more fully as itself.

To the spirit of Rasa Forever – felt rather than explained, to experience rather than conclude.

To the spaces that held these reflections – rooms, windows, thresholds of thought – where attention softened enough for something subtle to take form.

And to the reader – for entering this horizon not as one to understand, but as one who is met.